AF429015

Hex codes, or hexadecimal codes, are a way to represent colors in digital devices and web design. Each hex code refers to a very specific color. A hex color is expressed as a six-digit combination of numbers and letters, preceded by a pound sign or hashtag, defined by its mix of red, green, and blue (RGB). The first two letters or numbers refer to red, the next two refer to green, and the last two refer to blue.

The color values are defined as values between 00 and FF. Hex codes are a universal way to describe colors. This book is specifically about shades of gray.

A is for antique gray

A

#A5A9A0

a is for ash

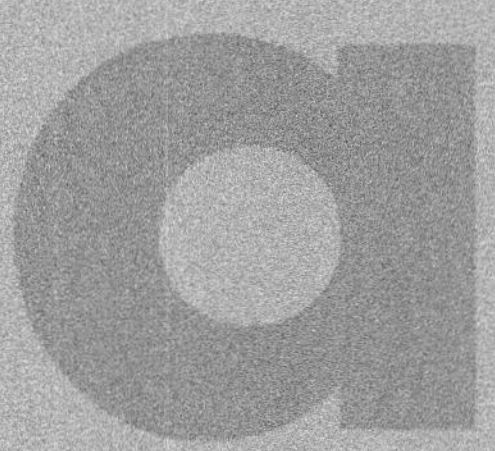

#B2BEB5

B is for basalt

B

#848482

b is for bombay

b

#AFB1B8

C is for celeste

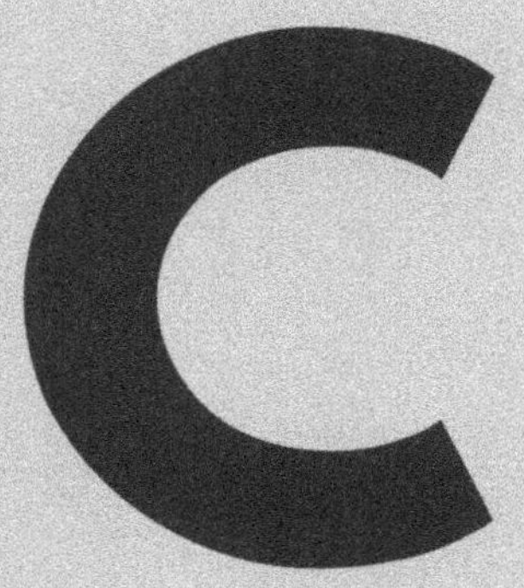

#D1D2CA

c is for chicago

C

#5D5C56

E is for edward

E

#A2AEAB

e is for electric

e

#55534F

F is for flotsam

F

#C8C4C0

f is for friar gray

f

#807E79

G is for ghost

G

#C7C9D5

g is for gray chateau

g

#A2AAB3

H is for heather

H

#B7C3D0

h is for hermitage

h

#B1B9B4

I is for infinity

I

#6A7376

i is for instinct

#8C979D

J is for jubilee grey

#7C7379

j is for jumbo

#7C7B82

K is for kangaroo

K

#C6C8BD

k is for kohl dust

k

#4A4A4B

L is for light slate gray

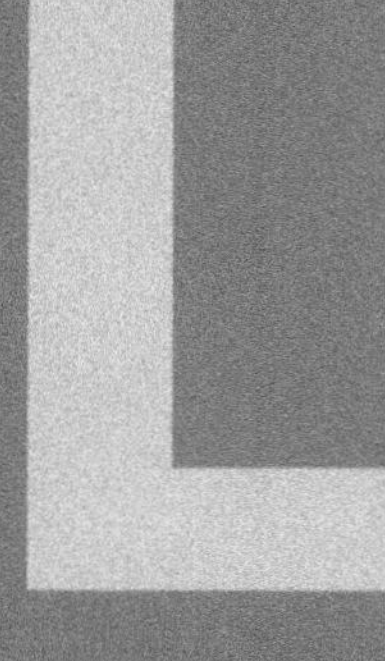

#778899

I is for loblolly

I

#BDC9CE

N is for neutral bay

N

#858D99

n is for nevada

n

#646E75

O is for oslo gray

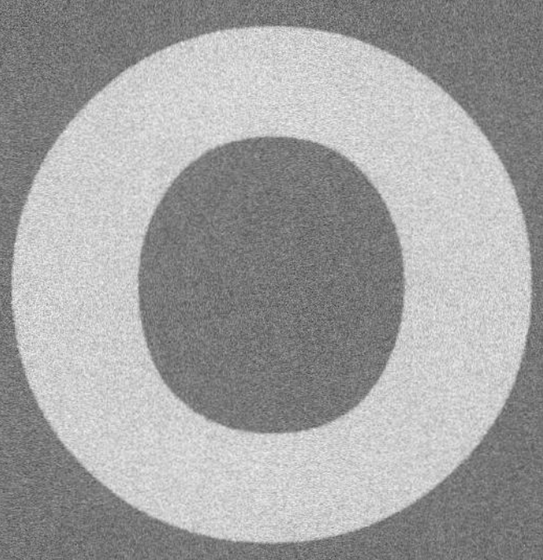

#878D91

o is for oxygen

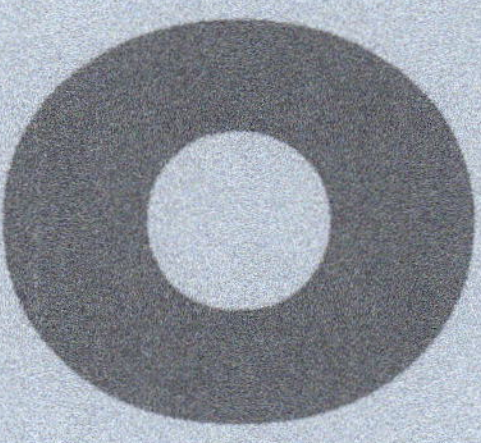

#BBC6D5

P is for pewter

P

#96A8A1

p is for pumice

p

#C2CAC4

Q is for quiet willow metal

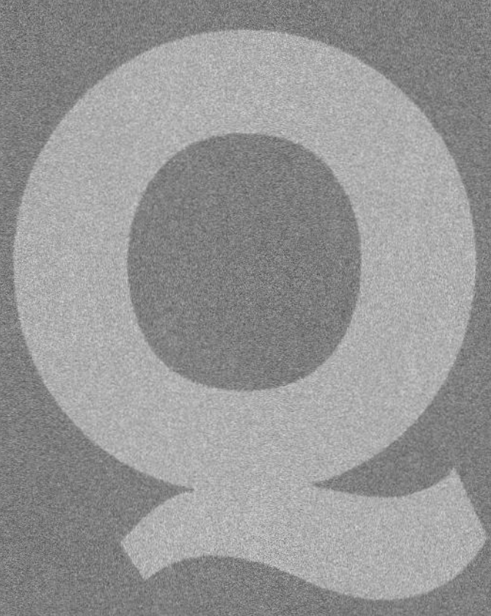

#8B8B82

q is for quincy granite

q

#B3B2AD

R is for riverstone

R

#797067

r is for rocket metallic

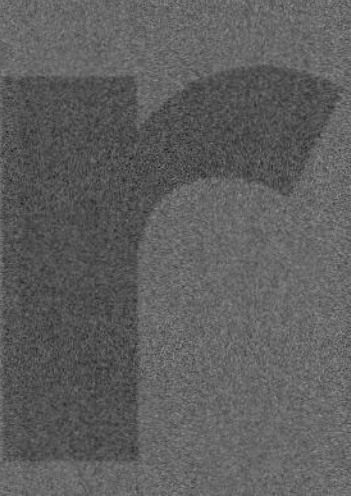

#8A7F80

S is for star dust

S

#9F9F9C

s is for sword

s

#808284

T is for tarmac

#6F6F6E

t is for trolley grey

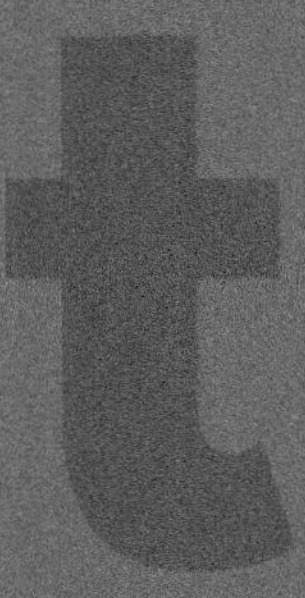

#808080

U is for universal grey

U

#C8C8C8

u is for urbane

#D9D1CF

V is for velvet gray

V

#ACAAB3

v is for viola ice gray

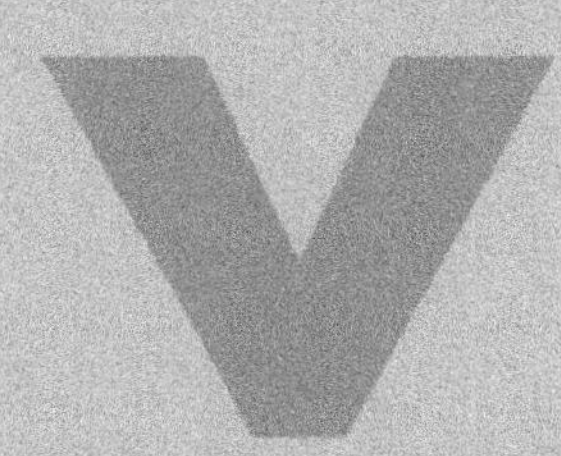

#C6C8D0

W is for weathered grey

W

#776F6F

w is for whiteout

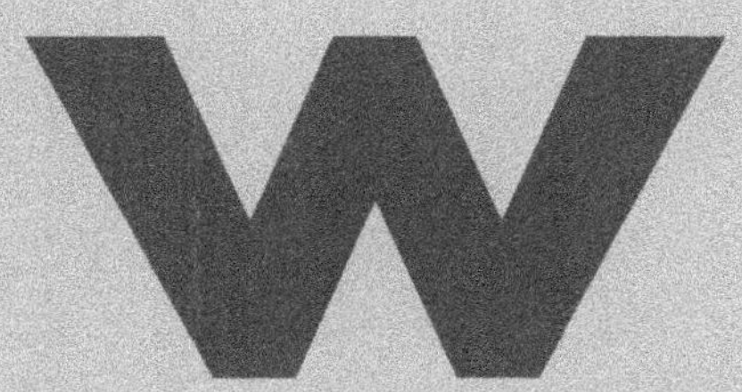

#CECAC8

X is for xl champagne metallic

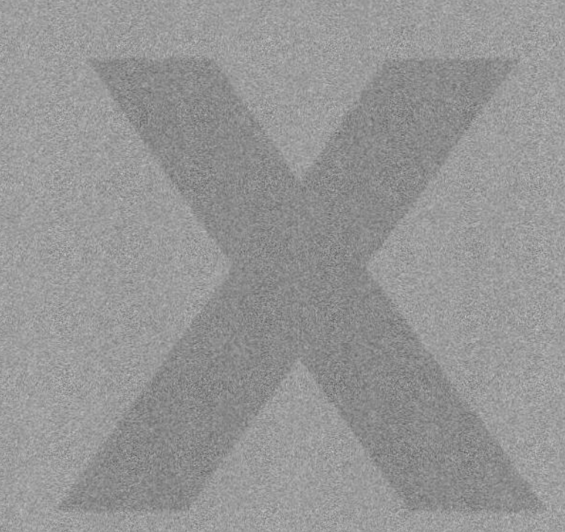

#A7A8A5

x is for xl telegray ii

#94989A

Y is for yachtsman

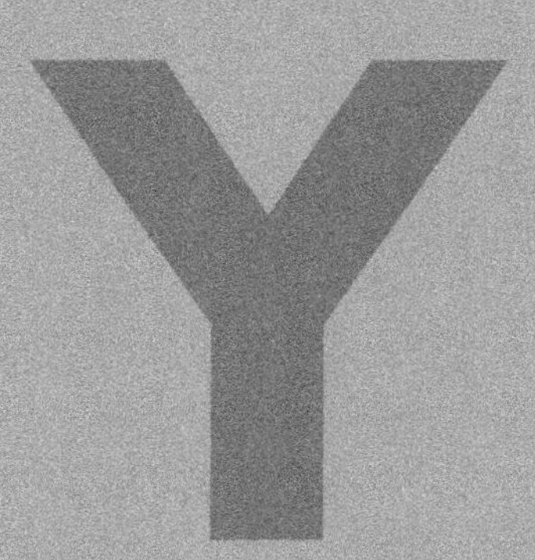

#AAB3B2

y is for yarmouth gray

y

#8C8D8D

Z is for zero gravity

Z

#BFC4C4

z is for zippered gray

z

#B0B5B9